Irish Americans

MARGARET C. HALL

Heinemann Library
Chicago, Illinois

Created by the publishing team at Heinemann Library
Designed by Roslyn Broder
Photo research by Amor Montes de Oca
Printed and Bound in the United States by Lake Book Manufacturing, Inc.

07 06 05 04 03
10 9 8 7 6 5 4 3 2 1

Library of Congress Cataloging-in-Publication Data
Hall, Margaret, 1947-
   Irish Americans / M.C. Hall.
     p. cm. — (We are America)
   Summary: Describes the conditions in Ireland that led people
to immigrate to the United States and what their daily lives are
like in their new home.
   Includes bibliographical references (p.) and index.
   ISBN 1-40340-734-7 (lib. bdg.) ISBN 1-40343-135-3 (pbk. bdg.)
   1. Irish Americans—Juvenile literature. 2. Immigrants—United States—Juvenile literature.
3. United States—Emigration and immigration—Juvenile literature. 4. Ireland—Emigration
and immigration—Juvenile literature. 5. Irish Americans—Biography—Juvenile literature.
6. Immigrants—United States—Biography—Juvenile literature.
   [1. Irish Americans.]   I. Title. II.Series.
   E184.I6 H35 2003
   973'.049162—dc21
   2002013098

Acknowledgments
The author and publishers are grateful to the following for permission to reproduce copyright material: pp. 4, 23, 27 Bettmann/Corbis; p. 5 AP Wide World Photos; pp. 6, 8, 10, 15, 17 Hulton Archive/Getty Images; p. 9 American Antiquarian Society; pp. 11, 12, 13, 14, 29 The Granger Collection; pp. 18, 28 Corbis; p. 19 U.S. National Archives & Records Administration; p. 20 Berneice Abbott/The Museum of the City of New York; p. 21 Jacob Riis/The Museum of the City of New York; p. 22 Heinemann Library; p. 24 Chicago Historical Society; p. 25 Chris Hondros/Liaison/Getty Images; p. 26 Tim Boyle/Liaison/Getty Images

Cover photographs by (foreground) Bettmann/Corbis, (background) Corbis

Special thanks to Director William Cobert and Special Projects Assistant Edward F. O'Reilly of the American Irish Historical Society for their comments in preparation of this book.

Some quotations and material used in this book come from the following sources. In some cases, quotes have been abridged for clarity: p. 21 *The Life Stories of Undistinguished Americans, As Told by Themselves* by Hamilton Holt (New York: Routledge, 1999).

Every effort has been made to contact copyright holders of any material reproduced in this book. Any omissions will be rectified in subsequent printings if notice is given to the publisher.

Some words are shown in bold, **like this.** You can find out what they mean by looking in the glossary.

On the cover of this book, an immigrant family from County Cork, Ireland, is shown in New York City on December 2, 1929. In the background, Canal Street in New Orleans, Louisiana, which was near a large Irish-American neighborhood, is shown in the late 1800s.

Contents

A New Home

Patrick Kennedy was born in 1823 near New Ross, Ireland. He was the youngest of nine children. The Kennedys had enough money to rent a farm. However, the farm was not big enough to support such a large family. There were few good jobs in Ireland. Because of this, many people had already left New Ross to go to the United States. They sent letters telling how much better life was there.

The house in which Patrick Kennedy grew up still stands in New Ross, Ireland, today.

Patrick decided to go the United States to find work. In 1849, he boarded a ship for the 40-day journey to Boston, Massachusetts. He had just enough money to pay for a ticket and a place to live until he found work. He didn't know it then, but one of his **descendants** would be remembered in history as a great American.

In 1963, U.S. President John F. Kennedy gave a speech near where Patrick Kennedy, his great-grandfather, left Ireland for the United States.

No country contributed more to building my own [country] than your sons and daughters.
—John F. Kennedy, speaking in Ireland in 1963

Ireland

For hundreds of years, people fought about who owned the land in Ireland. They also fought about religion. The **Protestant** Irish wanted to keep ties with England and make their religion the most important. Irish **Catholics** wanted to keep their own religion and **culture.** After battles in 1690 and 1691, England gained greater control of Ireland. Laws were passed that tried to get rid of Irish culture and to prevent Catholics from gaining power in Ireland.

This photo shows a family in front of a farmhouse in Ireland in about 1880.

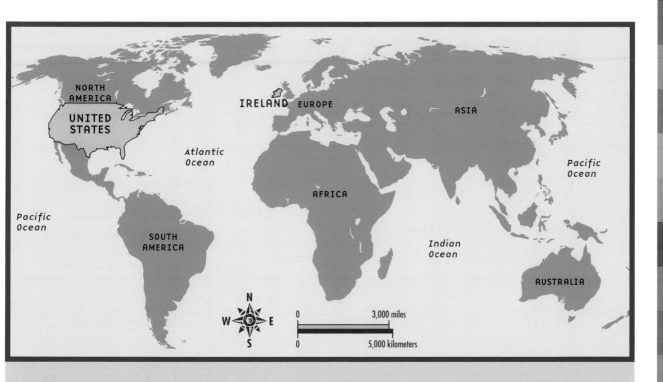

This map shows where Ireland and the United States are located in the world.

The laws also made it hard for Irish Catholics to own land. Most farmland was given to rich English people and wealthy Irish Protestants. In Ireland, farmers had to pay rent to use farmland. If a farmer did not pay, his family was thrown out of their home. People who did have land to farm were very poor. Many even had to beg for food. Many Irish people started looking for a way to live a better life.

The First Irish Americans

The Irish began coming to America as soon as England had **colonies** there. Some were Irish soldiers in England's army. Others came as **indentured servants.** They promised to repay the cost of the trip by working for years without pay. Some were **criminals.** Their punishment was being sent to work in the colonies.

United States presidents Andrew Jackson and Ronald Reagan traced their family histories and found they were descendants of early Irish immigrants.

*During the **Revolutionary War,** about half of the soldiers in America's army were Irish immigrants or their descendants.*

Time Line

Before 1600	Irish soldiers and workers come to the New England colonies.
1703	England begins sending criminals to the colonies.
1700s	Scotch-Irish immigrants **settle** in New England, Virginia, North Carolina, and South Carolina.
1841–1860	About two million Irish immigrants come to the United States after Ireland's potato crop fails.
1860–1865	Immigration slows because of the **Civil War**.
1870–1890	More than one million Irish immigrants arrive in the U.S.

During the 1700s, many **immigrants** who went to America called themselves "Scotch-Irish." They were **descendants** of people sent from Scotland to Ireland to start **Protestant** colonies. Many decided to leave Ireland because they did not get along with **Catholics.**

*This drawing shows Philadelphia, Pennsylvania, in 1799. The city was a major **port** city and had a large Irish population.*

Life in America

Most **indentured servants** worked as farmhands. After three to seven years, they earned their freedom. Many then moved west to farm on land that had not been **settled** yet. Some worked as trappers and guides. A trapper caught animals and sold their furs for people to wear.

Some Irish immigrants, like this trapper shown in 1850, worked in the wilderness and settled in the southern colonies.

This picture shows part of the Erie Canal in 1838 in Lockport, New York. Most of the Irish immigrants who helped build the canal had been farmers in Ireland.

Most American **colonists** were English **Protestants.** In 1636, a ship carrying Irish immigrants reached Boston. Some colonists tried to keep the Irish people from getting off the ship.

The next Irish who came to the United States were poor and usually had not gone to school for many years. They took whatever jobs they could find. From 1818 to 1825, many Irish **immigrants** helped dig the Erie **Canal.** The canal was a waterway built to connect New York's Hudson River to Lake Ontario.

More Irish Immigrants

In 1845, a disease struck Ireland's potato crop. Potatoes rotted in the ground. The disease spread through southern and western Ireland. It spoiled the crop for four years in a row. Without potatoes, many Irish families had very little food to eat. They had no crop to sell to get money to pay their rent. Some **landlords** tried to help by lowering rents. Others forced families to leave their homes as soon as they could not pay.

This painting shows poor people in Ireland receiving free clothing the year after Ireland's potato crop spoiled.

*The ships that the **immigrants** took to the United States were usually crowded. This painting shows what it might have looked like on a ship's deck.*

For many people, the only way to survive was to go to the United States. The trip often began with an "American **wake.**" Friends and family gathered as they did when someone died. They told stories, sang songs, and said good-bye.

Between 1841 and 1861, more than two million people died or left Ireland.

A Difficult Journey

Most **immigrants** started their trip by walking to **port** cities in Ireland or England. Ships that brought goods from North America to sell were willing to carry passengers on the way back. The trip was long and dangerous. Travelers often had to bring enough food to last for the four to eight weeks it took to reach North America. They were crowded into small, dark spaces where there were no toilets or beds.

Some Irish immigrants spent their time during the trip to the United States dancing and playing music, as this picture from 1850 shows.

This drawing from 1870 shows immigrants in the small, cramped rooms they had to sleep in on the ships.

Sickness spread quickly on the crowded ships. Fires and storms sometimes caused ships to sink. So many immigrants died on the way to North America that the ships were called coffin ships. The Irish immigrants who survived the trip sometimes headed to Canada, which was then an English **colony.** Some got off the ships in Boston or New York instead and stayed there.

Herman Melville, an American writer, worked on an immigrant ship. In his book *Redburn,* he wrote that the immigrants were "stowed away like bales of cotton."

The Arrival

In the 1800s, most **immigrants** arrived in **port** cities like New York and Boston. Other port cities were Philadelphia, Pennsylvania; Savannah, Georgia; and New Orleans, Louisiana. In 1855, Castle Garden opened in New York. It was a place where immigrants got off the ships to enter the United States. At Castle Garden, they could buy food and train tickets for fair prices. They could also find out about jobs and places to live.

*These are areas in the United States where Irish immigrants first came to and where many of their **descendants** still live today.*

Irish Immigration to the United States

When Castle Garden, shown above, opened in 1855, New York was the only city on the East Coast of the United States that had a special welcoming building for immigrants.

By 1890, Castle Garden was too small. A new building that immigrants had to go through when they came to the United States was opened on Ellis Island. On January 1, 1892, the first immigrant to arrive there was 15-year-old Annie Moore from Ireland. By the time Ellis Island closed in 1954, one million Irish immigrants had followed her.

Finding Work

Most Irish **immigrants** did hard work. They built roads, dams, railroads, and factories. They dug ditches and worked in coal mines. Many women and children went to work in factories where cloth and thread were made.

In Holyoke, Massachusetts, Irish immigrants built a dam and dug **canals** to carry water to mills. They also built the mills. By 1855, one out of every three people in Holyoke was Irish.

Some Irish immigrants worked in the western United States, like these men shown at a copper mine in Nevada.

These Irish immigrants, seen in 1882, dug clams from beaches in Boston, Massachusetts, and sold them for people to eat.

In 1849, when thousands of Irish immigrants were coming to the United States, gold was discovered in California. Men who could afford the trip went west, hoping to find gold and make a lot of money. Most ended up working in the mines for low pay.

Four Irish immigrants bought shares in a silver mine. It was the Comstock Lode, which became the most valuable silver mine in America.

Home in the City

Most Irish **immigrants settled** in large cities on the East Coast of the United States, such as New York, Boston, and Philadelphia. Life in the city was hard. Entire families often lived in one small room. There were no bathrooms or running water and little fresh air.

The only buildings that many Irish immigrants could afford to live in were often in poor shape, like the buildings shown here in Brooklyn, New York, in 1936.

Thousands of Irish immigrants settled in New York City, like these children shown there in 1890.

Many immigrants sent money back to family members in Ireland so someone else could make the trip. Whole families came to the United States one or two at a time. Although life was difficult, most Irish Americans survived and did well in the United States.

Immigrants Annie and Tilly McNabb worked and saved until they had enough money to bring their brothers to America. Then the sisters and brothers brought their parents from Ireland. Annie said: "We rented a little house . . . There was a parlor in it and kitchen . . . and marble door step, and a bell. To think of mother having a parlor and marble steps and a bell!"

Problems in the United States

Some Americans worried because so many Irish **immigrants** were coming to the United States. The immigrants were willing to work for low pay. Americans were afraid that their bosses would also pay them less, or that they would hire immigrants instead. Some businesses would not hire any Irish workers. Newspaper advertisements and help-wanted signs read, "No Irish need apply."

This sign is a modern recreation of the signs that used to appear in some cities in United States. Many immigrants were treated unfairly and could not get jobs simply because they were Irish.

HELP WANTED
NO IRISH NEED APPLY

FULTON STREET SIGN CO.

OCTOBER 12, 1916

*On July 12, 1871, a fight broke out on the streets of New York City between Irish Catholics and **Protestants.** Protestants had gathered for a Protestant celebration, and Catholics wanted to stop the event. About 50 people were killed or hurt.*

Sometimes, people were hit or called names just for being Irish and **Catholic.** In 1834, some people in Charleston, Massachusetts, set a Catholic school building on fire. Many Irish children went to school there. The people who burned the building thought that Irish Catholics should not be allowed into the United States.

Working Together

Irish Americans worked together to make life in the United States easier. In 1836, Irish Americans formed a Hibernian Society in New York City. The group was formed to keep Irish **Catholic traditions** alive. These groups were common in Ireland. Soon, Irish Americans in other cities started their own groups.

Irish **immigrants** *started clubs in the United States to celebrate Irish history and traditions. Members of the Irish Fellowship Club are shown here at a club dinner in 1909.*

In New York City, a group that is made up of Irish-American police officers marches in the St. Patrick's Day parade every year.

Working in **politics** was another way that Irish Americans helped themselves. In the 1800s, Irish men became American citizens so they could vote. When they helped to elect a city government leader, they were often rewarded with jobs. Many joined police forces and fire departments. Some even became city government leaders themselves.

In 1920, Ireland was divided into two parts. The northern part continued to be ruled by England. It became known as Northern Ireland. The southern part declared **independence** in 1949 and became the Republic of Ireland. Today, there is still violent fighting in Northern Ireland about religion and about how Northern Ireland should be run.

Irish-American Traditions

Today, most large cities in the United States have places where people can enjoy **traditional** Irish music, dancing, and food. Some Irish dishes include Irish stew, a thick soup with meat and vegetables, and shepherd's pie, which is a pie made with meat and mashed potatoes.

In the fifth century, Irish pirates caught an English boy named Patrick. He escaped and returned to England, where he became a **priest.** Later, he came back to Ireland to teach the people about the **Catholic** religion. Today, he is known as Saint Patrick.

These girls performed a traditional Irish dance in a St. Patrick's Day parade in Chicago, Illinois, in 2000.

Food dye is used every year to turn the Chicago River green in honor of St. Patrick's Day.

Every March 17, millions of Americans celebrate Saint Patrick's Day. There are parades with Irish dancers and musicians. Parade watchers shout "Erin go braugh," which means "Ireland forever" in the Irish language. New York City has the country's largest St. Patrick's Day parade. But many other cities also celebrate with special events. In Chicago, they even dye the Chicago River green for the day!

Patrick Kennedy's Story

There are no known pictures of Patrick Kennedy. This is a photo of his son, Patrick Joseph Kennedy, taken in about 1880.

Soon after he arrived in Boston, Massachusetts, in 1849, Patrick Kennedy married Bridget Murphy. She had also traveled from New Ross, Ireland, to Boston. Like many Irish **immigrants,** Patrick had dreamed of starting a farm in the United States. Instead, he found work making barrels that were used on ships. Later, his brother came to Boston and started a grocery store. Patrick went to work for him.

Patrick and Bridget had five children. In 1858, Patrick became ill with a fever. He died in November at the age of 35. His youngest son, Patrick Joseph, was only a baby. In 1960, Patrick Kennedy's great-grandson, John Fitzgerald Kennedy, became president of the United States. John F. Kennedy was the first Irish **Catholic** ever to be elected president.

More than 100 years after his great-grandfather came to the United States, John F. Kennedy was elected president of the United States.

We need men who can dream of things that never were.
—John F. Kennedy, in a speech he gave in Dublin, Ireland, in 1963

Irish Immigration Chart

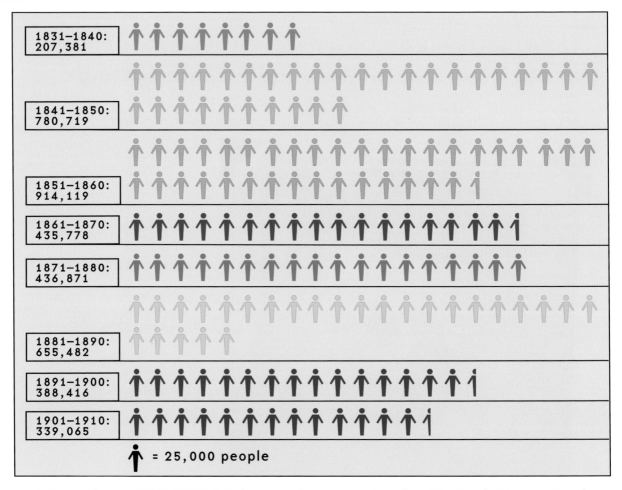

1831–1840: 207,381	↑↑↑↑↑↑↑↑
1841–1850: 780,719	↑↑↑↑↑↑↑↑↑↑↑↑↑↑↑↑↑↑↑↑↑↑↑↑↑↑↑↑↑↑↑
1851–1860: 914,119	↑↑↑↑↑↑↑↑↑↑↑↑↑↑↑↑↑↑↑↑↑↑↑↑↑↑↑↑↑↑↑↑↑↑↑↑
1861–1870: 435,778	↑↑↑↑↑↑↑↑↑↑↑↑↑↑↑↑↑↑
1871–1880: 436,871	↑↑↑↑↑↑↑↑↑↑↑↑↑↑↑↑↑↑
1881–1890: 655,482	↑↑↑↑↑↑↑↑↑↑↑↑↑↑↑↑↑↑↑↑↑↑↑↑↑↑
1891–1900: 388,416	↑↑↑↑↑↑↑↑↑↑↑↑↑↑↑↑
1901–1910: 339,065	↑↑↑↑↑↑↑↑↑↑↑↑↑↑

↑ = 25,000 people

More than 900,000 Irish people came to the United States in the years 1851 to 1860.

Source: U.S. Immigration and Naturalization Service

More Books to Read

Allan, Tony. *The Irish Famine: The Birth of Irish America.* Chicago: Heinemann Library, 2001.

O'Hara, Megan. *Irish Immigrants, 1840–1920.* Mankato, Minn.: Capstone Press, 2002.

Parker, Lewis K. *Why Irish Immigrants Came to America.* New York: Rosen Publishing, 2003.

Glossary

canal ditch dug and filled with water so that boats can cross a stretch of land. Canals are also used to get water to crops.

Catholic member of the Roman Catholic Church, the religion led by the pope that follows teachings of the Bible

Civil War war fought in 1861 to 1865 between groups from the North and the South of the United States

colony territory that is owned or ruled by another country

criminal person who breaks the law

culture ideas, skills, arts, and way of life for a certain group of people

descendant person who has come from a particular older person or family

immigrate to come to a country to live there for a long time. A person who immigrates is an immigrant.

independent condition of being free from the rule of other countries, governments, or people. The state of being independent is called independence.

indentured servant person who agrees to work for an employer for free for a certain amount of time to repay a debt

landlord person who owns land or buildings that they rent to others

politics activities that have to do with leading a city, state, or nation

port city near water where ships dock and leave from

priest spiritual leader of Catholic religion

Protestant member of a Christian church other than the Catholic

Revolutionary War war from 1775 to 1783 between the thirteen American colonies and Great Britain

settle to make a home for yourself and others

tradition belief or practice handed down through the years from one generation to the next

wake gathering of family and friends when someone dies

Index